My Skin Is Me

Travis Saint Julian

Illustrated by Henry Lewis

NEWMAN SPRINGS PUBLISHING
320 Broad Street
Red Bank, NJ 07701

First originally published by Newman Springs Publishing 2024

ISBN 979-8-89061-729-3 (Paperback)
ISBN 979-8-89061-730-9 (Digital)

Printed in the United States of America

To Theresa, Juno, Catherine, and Paul

What a beautiful day

Spent Under a tree

1

2

3

People as far as the eye can see

So many shades and colors
Not just two or three

5

I Love my skin
My skin is me

Hug someone that doesn't look like you

At least once a day, and some days two

I Love it Because Your Skin Is you

Some skin is pale
Like a white dough bun

13

Some skin is tanned
Kissed by the sun

15

Some skin is dark
   Like Chocolate cake
The more shades you know
   The more friends you make

Freckled, speckled

Dark, and pale

Chocolate, cream, and caramel

21

A big **hurray**
For different skin
That come together
For the win !

This is the way the world should be:
Love you for you,
And me for me

23

24

A world united is meant to be
I love my skin, my skin is me